GHOSTWAYS

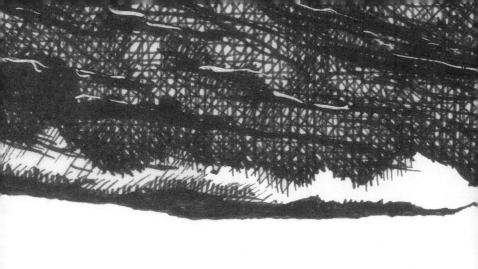

ROBERT MACFARLANE,

STANLEY DONWOOD,

and DAN RICHARDS

GHOSTWAYS

Two Journeys in Unquiet Places

W. W. NORTON & COMPANY
Independent Publishers Since 1923

Ness first published in the UK by Quive-Smith Editions 2018, first published by
Hamish Hamilton 2019
Holloway first published in the UK by Quive-Smith Editions 2012, first published
by Faber & Faber Ltd 2013, Faber & Faber Ltd paperback first published 2014

First American Edition 2020

For information about permission to reproduce selections from this book, write to
Permissions, W. W. Norton & Company, Inc., 500 Fifth Avenue, New York, NY 10110

For information about special discounts for bulk purchases, please contact
W. W. Norton Special Sales at specialsales@wwnorton.com or 800-233-4830

Manufacturing by Lake Book Manufacturing
Production manager: Beth Steidle

ISBN: 978-1-324-01582-6 (pbk.)

W. W. Norton & Company, Inc., 500 Fifth Avenue, New York, N.Y. 10110
www.wwnorton.com

W. W. Norton & Company Ltd., 15 Carlisle Street, London W1D 3BS

1 2 3 4 5 6 7 8 9 0

Contents

Foreword

The Irish phrase *Áiteanna Tanaí* – usually translated as 'thin places', or 'places of the shade' – refers to those landscapes in which the past is eerily restless, or the thresholds between realms are slender. The book you hold in your hands tells two stories of two such places. In keeping with their unsettled subjects, *Ness* and *Holloway* both shift between forms, and both are the work of more than one maker. Both were written in part to be read aloud, or at least sounded in the mind's ear – and also to flash upon the eye in their mixing of word and image. In them, 'landscape' is not a smooth surface or simple stage set, there to offer picturesque consolations; rather it is complexly constituted by uncanny forces, part-buried conflicts and strange animisms.

Ness takes place in a version of Orford Ness, the ten-mile-long shingle spit that lies off the coast of East Anglia, shaped and reshaped by storm, tide and longshore drift. For seventy years (1913–1983) this isolated "untrue island" was used by the British Ministry of Defence to conduct secret weapons tests: from air gunnery and bombing during the First World War, through to the stress-testing of nuclear weapons in the 1950s and '60s. There is no English landscape that has come to fascinate me more than the Ness, or to disrupt my usual ways of seeing. Produced by a collision of human death drive and natural life, it is unnerving in its juxtapositions: decaying ferro-concrete laboratories are recolonised by moss, bracken and elder to become 'green chapels'; black-backed gulls build their nests in broken control panels; brown hares big as deer lope across expanses of shingle cratered by explosions, and the wind sings in the wires of abandoned perimeter fences.

Holloway takes place in a deep-sunk lane in Dorset, near the south coast of England; a 'hollowed way' used by walkers and riders for so many centuries that it has become worn far down into the soft golden bedrock of the region. Such hollo-ways have long served as refuges; for recusant Catholics fleeing persecution in the sixteenth and seventeenth centuries; for wild creatures seeking shelter from intensive farming and human interference; and for individuals who wish to slip out of the present for a while. I first explored the Dorset holloways early in the 2000s with a dear friend called Roger Deakin. Roger died not long afterwards, far too young, and ever since these sunken lanes – where time loops, folds and echoes – have been haunted sites for me, to which I have frequently returned, including with *Holloway*'s coauthors, the writer Dan Richards and the artist Stanley Donwood.

A recurring image in *Ness* is the 'hagstone'; a flint pebble with a hole worn naturally through it. In folklore across Europe, to look through such a stone is to see into the future, the past or the afterlife. *Ghostways* holds a hagstone up to landscape, and shows the skulls beneath its skin.

—*Robert Macfarlane, 2020*

Ness

AWRE/6/79

QV 06 79 76D/00

WE-177A

Look – five forms moving fast through the forests to Ness.

Look – here *it* comes, its bones are plastic, it builds itself from pallet slat & bottle-top, rises from sift, is lashed & trussed with fishing line. It is drift: it has cuttlefish nails & sea-poppy horns, it breathes in rain & it breathes out rust.

Look – here *he* comes, his bones are willow & he sings in birds. He rises in marsh, slips forwards by ripple & shiver. Between his tree-ribs birds flutter, then swoop ahead to settle, sing, quiver. His head is a raven's, his eyes are wrens' nests. By day from his throat fly finch & fire-crest & in anger he speaks only in swifts.

Look – here *she* comes, her skin is lichen & her flesh is moss & her bones are fungi, she breathes in spores & she moves by hyphae. She is a rock-breaker, a tree-speaker, a place-shaper, a world-maker.

Look – here *they* come, their eyes are hagstones & their words are shingle. They rise on the shore, rock-cored, flint beings, scattering chert to signal their passage, sending stones through time to foretell their seeings.

Look – here *as* comes, who exists only as likeness, moves as mist & also as metal, cannot be grasped or forced, is the strongest & strangest & youngest & oldest of all the five, slipping through trees, past houses, rolled by the wind at years each minute – rolled by the wind as if through time & in it.

it, he, she, they, as

All five know where they must go &

with what they must grapple &

where they must go is to the Green Chapel

Listen. Listen now. Listen to Ness.

Ness speaks. Ness speaks gull, speaks wave, speaks bracken & lapwing, speaks bullet, ruin, gale, deception.

Ness speaks pagoda, transmission, reception, Ness speaks pure mercury, utmost secret, swift current, rapid-fire.

Listen again. Listen back. Listen to the pasts of Ness. Listen inland to the long-gone wood, which rings with the cries of *wildcat & brock, heorte & hind, doe & bocke, hare & fox, wild fowle with his flocke, patrich, pheasant hen & pheasant cock, with green & wild stub & stock.*

Listen to the wrench of the door in the Centrifuge Dome. Listen to the rise of the still encroaching ocean. Listen to the silence of the merman who *would not talk, e'en when tortured & hung up by his feete.* Listen to the rumoured motion of the rumoured bodies on the rumoured shore.

Shut up & listen, though, will you? Really listen. What the fuck is that, coming from the Green Chapel?

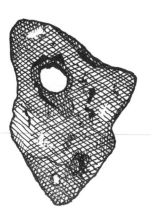

IN THE GREEN CHAPEL

I

The Armourer says:

Who will describe the Chapel's design and position?

'I,' says The Engineer.

'Ten tall thin crosses on the west wall, and ten on the east.
Five on the north – and the south wall is open.
Its status as a building of worship is unmistakable, so too
    the nature of its god.
Its roof is ferro-concrete and strikingly vaulted.
Its pillars are ferro-concrete and devoid of fluting.
Its architecture is a perfect marriage of function and
    form.
It lies close to the Centrifuge, close to the Armoury,
And its ruination is controlled.'

The Armourer says:

Who will describe the Chapel's ornament and flourish?

'I,' says The Botanist, looking thoughtfully around.

'Elder and bracken thrive on its outer walls.

Shingle fills the nave and the transept.

Gulls have built nests in our control panels, whose doors
hang open, whose springs loll, whose dials tilt.

Its lichens and its mosses are fascinatingly many, though
I will not detain you with their Linnaeans now.'

The Armourer says:

Do not. Tell me instead: is the Chapel fit for our purpose?

'It is,' says The Botanist.

The Armourer says:

Who will number the congregation?

'I,' says The Ornithologist, stepping forwards and bowing to
The Armourer before speaking.

'Our congregation numbers the gulls, the black-backs,
who have travelled so very far to be here with us
today.

Our congregation numbers the ghosts of those who
worked here to make today possible, including the
indentured Chinese labourers who kept grasshop-
pers in jars to remind them of home, and the German
POWs who raised their voices in song.

Our congregation numbers the curlew and the brown
hare, the fishermen, sailors and lighthouse keepers,
the water deer, the foxes and the swaying valerian ...'

The Armourer cuts across The Ornithologist, says:

Enough of your pieties. Who will take the service in the
Chapel?

'I will,' says The Physicist, stepping forwards in his greatcoat,
though curiously his feet make no noise on the shingle that
increasingly fills the nave and the transept.

'I intend in the service to speak only in equations, for
they are the purest of utterances and they address
only the world of matter, and they have no correl-
ate or purchase in the sphere of politics and yet
they possess a vast and calculable power to alter the
world we inhabit.'

The Armourer says:

Physicists have long flattered themselves thus, and I see you
continue the tradition. Nevertheless I thank you all for
your work and preparation. We are ready to bring in the
bomb to complete its trajectory.

The Engineer and The Physicist go into the narthex and wheel
out of it a long green gurney, on which is laid a toothpaste-white
finned missile a little longer than a man. WE-177A – for this
is the missile's name – is banded twice round with yellow and
once round with red.

The Armourer says:

Let us sing 'The Firing Song'.

They all begin to sing in a cracked chorus, and then further voices that do not seem to possess corresponding bodies join in with them:

> 'Oh happy band of pilgrims, look upward to the
> skies
> Where such a light affliction shall win so great a
> prize!
>
>> *Song of the bomb, the arming song,*
>> *the firing song …'*

It

It is Drift. Drift nears Ness. Drift is a world-shaper. Drift
makes itself up as it goes along.

Drift loves lists. Drift is tide, gravity, storm, waves,
wind, gyre & coastal aspect, among other things. Drift also
acknowledges its debts to the plastics & fishing industries, &
to the global capital flows that determine prevailing trade cur-
rents. Drift looks drastically disorganized to the untrained
eye but is in fact a micro-manager of obsessive-compulsive
tidiness. Drift's favourite holiday destination is two tiny
cove-beaches on the English south coast, one of which gathers right-handed gloves in its jetsam & the other of which
gathers left-handed gloves in its jetsam.

Drift is consistently underestimated by those who encounter it. Drift is frequently seen as lacking any clear direction
in life. Drift's school reports repeatedly drew attention to its
lack of commitment, its inability to settle on a single course
of action. Weary careers advisers submitted Drift to the usual
psychometric aptitude tests, which remarkably did not recom-
mend that Drift become either a prison warden or a zookeeper,
but nevertheless failed to conclude that Drift had a single clear

path in life. Afloat on the job market, however, Drift began quietly to impress in its various workplaces with its skills of improvisational spontaneity, untiring gathering, its devotion to habitat creation & its ecumenical readiness to admit all-comers to its care.

Drift is highly discriminatory but wholly without prejudice.

Drift relishes equally the company of sea-coal, Lego *Star Wars* figures, barnacles & gull feathers. Drift is fully reconciled to the unattached life. Drift has been known to unite shoes with long-lost partners & more generally to matchmake wholly unlikely relationships, but also to be the cause of unnumbered break-ups. Drift speaks an unpretentious tongue, a mongrel patois pâté of this-&-that, bodged into anyoldcreole.

When you're with Drift, *time* does really strange things. Drift is one of those friends who make sequence shiver, lay out odd things side by side, fully disassemble the normal for a while. Today with Drift is pre-Cambrian, today with Drift is Anthropocene.

Drift doesn't really do time, though – Drift more does space.

Drift is always becoming. Drift has unbounded potential. Drift is unimaginably vast & if you had to describe Drift you would need a new kind of map & a new kind of language. The only end to Drift would be the end of the oceans, which in turn would be the end of the planet – & no one really wants that.

When you're with Drift, *space* does really strange things. Drift is a hermit crab taking an Avon face-cream tub as its shell on a Pacific atoll. Drift is four hundred & thirty-four rusted steel fishing globe-floats in a single bay on a south-westerly island of the Lofoten archipelago. Drift is the wood out of which humans were first carved. Drift dislikes being made to represent anything, because Drift disapproves strongly of symbolism, allegory & indeed all systems of fungibility which devalue the glittering particularity of all that Drift makes. Drift is matter plus motion & that is the end of it.

Listening to Drift is one of the most beautiful sounds in the world, as beautiful as listening to your child breathe in the darkness.

Drift is an avocet skull writhing with maggots. Drift is a Colgate-Palmolive Teeth-Whitening Toothpaste tube, no top. Drift is a seal corpse with a zither-rig jaw & off-planet fur. Drift is kelp & bladderwrack. Drift is long-line hooks & seine net. Drift is jerrycan & doll's head, & Drift is a beached sperm whale, sheer-sided as a battleship, downwind of which you cannot stand, leaking red into the rocks, watching the world grey out through one tiny upwards eye.

Drift happens to you rather than you to Drift.

Right now, Drift is approaching Ness from the sea by all directions & Drift is coming in piece by piece, gathering on the upslope of the storm-beach, quietly assembling itself to either side of the Green Chapel without them noticing. The laboratories will be Drift soon − & Ness too, *owing to nothing but the fate of things.*

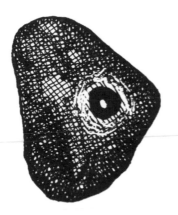

IN THE GREEN CHAPEL

II

The Armourer says:

Who will retell how we came to this historic moment, this momentous place?

'I will,' says The Physicist. 'It went something like this —

You near Ness from far inland: first you hit pine, then you hit sand, then the sky goes grey from the glare of the sea.

Ness is a place to improvise. Ness is its own realm with its own rules. Don't look. Don't tell. Don't understand. Don't ever remember. Wait at the quay, load up the boat, then Charon ferries you over to the island of secrets. Two flints on your eyes for the journey, cold on the lids, keeping sight in so you couldn't find your way back.

Out there then. Lonely, flat, old. East wind like a knife. Spartan, cold. Eerie for its absence of feature. The sea-birds cry, the spit moves in the storm like a creature.

We weren't much more than children. Quick minds gathered from all over the land, brought to this cold marsh, this locked-in place that shifts in its sleep, in our sleep. Sign the Act, don't talk about what you do, not even to each other.

For what we do is perfect the physics of death.
We test for lethality and
we test for vulnerability.

We shock-test, stress-test, shake-test, temperature-test.
We crash casings into concrete.

We spin detonators in the Centrifuge.
We heat initiator charges.

We store weapons in the Armoury.
In the Green Chapel
we simulate all that our
bombs will face when
the end times come.

We seek to maximize injuries incompatible with life.

How did we keep it all quiet, out there on the untrue island? Oh – with half-truths and full falsehoods. We bred speculation, suppressed revelation, formed and dispersed a thick mist of lie in which we ourselves wandered. And we came to love our bombs, our seven dwarfs with their Disney names:

Blue Danube
Blue Streak
Big Bertha
Brown Bunny
Blue Peacock
Blue Hare
Yellow Sun
(with its helical fins giving a beautiful spin to its fall).

And who could forget WE-177A – an ice-white stork-dropped messenger from heaven, with such a bright future ahead of it?

Oh – we sowed our signals and we reaped the air. We eavesdropped on Plesetsk by loop, Algiers by back-scatter; we tracked the flights of planes, the arcs of missiles, the paths of ships, the movements of trains.

But we also picked up what wasn't uttered. For this was the problem: the fissile sign, the answerless answer. How to sift the message from the clutter?'

The Armourer says:

That was well told. Very well told. Physicist, I thank you.

Now it is time to continue 'The Firing Song'.

Hollow voices rise in half-harmony:

'Oh happy band of pilgrims, drift upward to the skies
Where such a light affliction shall win so great a prize!

Song of the bomb, the drifting song,
the firing song.

Shingle shelters bunker, bunker shelters blast,
Dark drifts down, night rises fast.

Song of the bomb, the arming song,
the firing song.'

The Physicist glances across at The Engineer and tilts his head quizzically.

For The Physicist notices that one of The Engineer's pupils has become oddly mobile, that it seems to be drifting rapidly back and forth across the confines of its iris. The Engineer looks back, smiles unconcernedly, lost in the words of 'The Firing Song'.

The Physicist notices that The Engineer's other pupil is standing out slightly from his eyeball, like a buried plug of old grey metal.

The Physicist notices something else that he finds hard to scale or to understand. A pale green light has filled the Chapel except that this light seems only scantly to occupy the open air or to shine on the outer surfaces of the Chapel; rather it emanates somehow from *within* every solid object organic and inorganic now contained in the Chapel, including The Physicist himself, and somehow to condense on the inside of every visible surface, leaving only a trace radiance beyond that border, and even as The Physicist is trying to represent this phenomenon to himself in language he is simultaneously, furiously trying to reject the possibility of the phenomenon's existence within the realm of the real as he comprehends it.

He

He nears Ness. He moves through the marshes much as mud
might. You couldn't call it walking; this march matches no
known gait. He pours himself forwards; pours, sets, melts &
pours again, in a skipping looping flow, learnt part from otter
& part from water. Willow weaves in him, weaves him in: roots & leafs &
writhes, making & remaking his body's bones with cease-
less invention &, it must be said, a certain degree of arch
self-consciousness: four-boned plaited shins; a thirty-ribbed
sternum within which wood-cage shifts a throng of birds
whose song can be heard for miles in every direction –

Wrens' notes sharp as needles sewing thread.
Blackbirds chinking like pennies on glass.
Kew-kew scold of buzzards, clack of skua,
The godwit's call which is red-gold,
& ever the jag & haggle of the gulls.

So he pours himself noisily onwards through the woods &
through the marshes & along the beach to Ness. The Green
Chapel can be seen now & his birds are becoming excited.

Their songs now are no longer transparent single notes but bright lines looping silver through the air, lacing & flowing & webbing together above the Green Chapel. The willow in his chest – in his legs, in his hips – is weaving & unweaving faster & faster in anticipation.

From within him he can hear Oven-Bird & Hay-Jack, Mavis & Coddy-Moddy, Magareen, Fulfer & the Rain-Bird, all singing the high notes – the oversong.

From within him he can hear Butcher Bird & Blood Olf & his swifts (the bird which revels in the storm & is born of the hurricane, the bird which goes by several names & those are Deviling, Shriek-Devil, Howler & Screech-Owl; right in their darkness for what's gone on here) all singing the low notes – the undersong.

His two wrens fly from their nests in his raven-head sockets, to perch unseen on the upper edge of the Green Chapel, in the vaultings, bobbing & flicking & looking down with their bead-black eyes into what is happening in the transept below.

Above the Green Chapel his swifts are building & building in number, cutting the sky into screaming black sections with their wings.

IN THE GREEN CHAPEL

III

'Can you hear something?' asks The Ornithologist of no one in particular.

The Armourer says:

> *Let the catechism commence. Who holds the Strike Enable Facility keys for the operational round?*

'I do,' says The Engineer, holding up a pair of white plastic plugs and a cylindrical barrel key, tagged with a blue disc on which is marked by hand the number 75215.

The Armourer says:

> *Do we intend to detonate in shallow coastal waters in depths up to but not exceeding forty metres, or do we intend to detonate in deep oceanic waters at depths below forty metres?*

Chorally they reply: 'In shallow coastal waters.'

The Armourer says:

> *Then we must regretfully restrict ourselves to the 0.5-kilo-*
> *tonne yield.*
> *And have we in all ways, to the best of our specialisms and*
> *to the full extent of our expertise, given the dynamism of*
> *the situation, optimized both yield and kill probability?*

Chorally: 'We have.'

> *Then let us begin the detonation sequence. First we will arm*
> *the round.*

The Engineer steps eagerly forwards, uses one of the white plastic plugs to open the arming panel, and then – peering through
his changed eyes – fits the barrel key and turns it clockwise by
180 degrees. He seems surprised and a little disappointed by
the ease of this action. The Armourer looks pleased.

The Armourer says:

> *Let us sing 'The Firing Song'.*

They begin to sing again, but the words do not take form in air
entirely as they have been intended:

> 'Oh happy band of pilgrims, drift upward to the
>   skies
> Where such a murmuration shall win so great a
>   prize!
>
> > *Song of the bomb, the drifting song,*
> > *the firing song.*

Shingle shelters bunker, bunker shelters blast,
Dark drifts down, night flies fast.

> *Song of the wren, the devil-bird's song,*
> *the firing song.*

This half-life landscape fading to grey.
The king's in his cradle, the bomb's in its bay.'

The Physicist looks up into the vaultings of the Green Chapel. In the green light that is now both without and within his body — but that does not seem to pass through his skin or any other surface, rather to exist in separate domains on either side of a horizon, as if coming from two distinct sources — there are quick sharp shadows flickering faster and faster, on banking turns and orbits, shadows that are scythe-like and that, as he watches, cut towards him through the greenness and then pass into his body as if the greenness has somehow given them free entry or made him translucent, and he watches these shadows move within and through him at dazzling speeds, painless and graceful.

She

She nears Ness. Her skin is lichen & her flesh is moss & her bones are fungi & she breathes spores. Spores spread as she breathes out, sucked back into her gills with each deep breath in, gusted ahead with each deep breath out.

She is wired into the world. There are miles of her in a pinch of soil. Trees speak through her. As she passes houses, passes trees, passes cars, she leaves herself behind. Moss clump on roof tile, wall edge; lichen tag on road sign, fungus glowing on tree bark. Here & there she marks certain children as they sleep: a fingertip-touch on the inside of a wrist, the back of a knee, a place where green can enter & grow, making over time a child of moss, a child of ash, a child of beech, a child of lichen. She was one of them once & her skin now greenly seethes.

She is not green but she makes green. Colour is not a possessed property. You cannot see her if you look straight at her. Like the pigmentless fur of certain moles which turns light gold, though they have no life of light & no need of gold; like the feather-stream on a kingfisher's back which bends light through its barbs & splits it into blue water & blue jewels, she makes green & green fills the air around her & warps hard into objects within her radiance. She is not colour but a mixture of brightness & movement. If pressed, in certain company, she describes herself not as a subjective experience but as a relative object.

She is green above ground & she is white below, for she is moss & lichen but she is also fungi & hyphae, slipping through earth as easily as she steps through air & rising up in a riot after rain. She is committed to redefining decay as a form of verdancy, individuality as a biological aberration & gender as a parallax error or species anomaly. If she had to become another kind of organism or organisms, she would choose to be a siphonophore for its explosion of conventional notions of community. If you left her on a rock, given time, she would crack it with her acids.

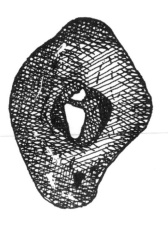

IN THE GREEN CHAPEL

IV

The Armourer says:

Recite the detonation sequence, taking care to emphasize its
causal beauty and irreversibility once commenced.

The Engineer answers mechanically, staring blindly towards
The Armourer through his iron eye (left) and his drifting eye
(right), through light that is now as green as underwater, within
which still move at impossible speeds the blade-shadows:

'Following release over the kill zone the drogue parachute
will deploy by means of explosive charge and ejection
gun. Four main parachutes will then deploy by means
of cutter charges. Hydrostatic fuses will then deploy.
The gas-motor-triggered clockwork timer is present
as back-up in the event of failure of the radar-trig-
gered airburst fuses. Saltwater sensors in the nose
cone will confirm water entry and track descent rate

and depth, before pressure sensors trigger the firing unit at a depth of around thirty-five metres.'

The Armourer says:

And then?

'Then the six-tile implosion device within its welded beryllium capsule within its stainless-steel cladding will implode.'

The Armourer says:

And then?

'Then the fission fuel begins its fission and the temperature consequently rises such that the fissile material enters a supercritical state, and thermonuclear fusion commences. Large numbers of neutrons are produced, striking other fissile nuclei, in turn releasing a much larger number of secondary neutrons, which in turn strike other fissile nuclei, and ... so on and so on. You get the idea.'

The Armourer says:

I get the idea. In fact, I sometimes like to think that I helped invent the idea. And then?

'Then the neutron shield reflects fleeing neutrons back into the physics package, intensifying the reaction. Fusion boosting using the hyper-energetic deuterium-tritium neutrons increases the rate and thus the yield of the thermonuclear reaction. There

will be some escape losses and scattering, of course,
but the fusion boosting will ensure a second genera-
tion of chain reaction.'

The Armourer says:

And then?

'Then the core explosively disassembles. Recognition life
extinct.'

The Armourer says:

Not before time.

'Actually, we might reasonably say "before time", because
the ultra-high velocity of the fusion neutrons leads to
what is called "time magnification".'

The Armourer says:

*Time magnification? Oh – I like the sound of that. Now for
the last time, let us sing 'The Firing Song'.*

The men sing with all that is left of their hearts:

'Oh happy band of pilgrims, drift upward to the
skies
Where such a murmuration shall win so great a
prize!
*Song of the bomb, the drifting song,
the firing song.*

Shingle shelters bunker, bunker shelters blast,
Dark drifts down, night flies fast.

> Song of the wren, the devil-bird's song,
> the firing song.

A lichenous landscape mossing to green.
The king's in his cradle, the bomb's in its bay.

> Song of the spores, the drifting song,
> the firing song.

Colour-band tightens from blue down to grey,
The final declension of world and of day.

> Song of the bomb, the arming song,
> the firing song.'

The Bryologist watches The Ornithologist's open mouth as he sings these words that are not the intended words. A bee that is, but cannot be, made of some kind of supple metal crawls out of one corner of The Ornithologist's mouth, and up his cheek to his forehead, where it crosses his hairline and then disappears wholly, as if entering a burrow. Another follows the same course, then another. It occurs to The Bryologist that they must be miner bees because their abdomens are red and because they are mining.

Moths are clustering and flocking softly in vast numbers around the bomb, settling on it first as snow might fall on land then as coccolithophores might rock to ocean floor, building up in depth, thorax to thorax and wing to wing, leaving tiny glittering squares of wing powder, until they reach such vibrant density that it seems to those in the Green Chapel that they might contain *anything*, block out *any* source of light, soften *any* blow.

The Bryologist looks at The Physicist's neck as he sings. From his lower jaws down to his collar The Physicist's skin is scaled with a bright orange lichen. The Bryologist by reflex identifies the species as *Xanthoria parietina*, a lichen that thrives in polluted air. He looks at The Physicist's hands and sees that they have become intricate with map-lichens, finely black-bordered cartographies of close-bound countries lacking any access to the sea, and he looks at his eyes and sees that there are fine branching white lines growing across his eyes, just below the surface.

'Armourer,' says The Physicist – though his words are hard to make out because they are spoken softly but with force, pushing through the emerald-green sphagnum moss that is now blooming plushly in his mouth – 'something is very wrong here.'

They

They are stone-deaf & sea-eyed & their calm is the deep calm
of deep time, the cold calm of cold time, & their closeness is old
as rock & ocean & their motion as ancient as wave & shore &
their rhythm is that of growth & erosion & you could not say
of them that they are several or single & they have flint in their
being & they send stones through time to foretell their seeing
& their speech is shingle.

    & they have the patience of granite & the ardour of lava &
the speed of starlight.

    & they are the white band that rings a blue-grey chert-stone
held in the hand for a minute & for longer in the heart.

    & they are the utter shattered matter at the outer limit of
all that the mind's gravity can hold in shape.

    & they can recite the colour phases of ice as it ages & deep-
ens from white flake to black star, though not in words that we
would understand.

    & if they can be said to think it might be figured as the
strange process of attraction whereby flint forms, the slow sili-
cate grammar-gather of flecks of entity, creeping together over
millennia.

& they have no need of watches for they keep time with tree-rings, with pollen grains, with the unvarying decay-rates of carbon-14 & uranium-235.

& time to them is not deep, not deep at all, for time is only ever overlapping tumbling versions of the now.

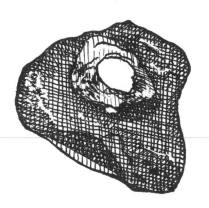

IN THE GREEN CHAPEL

V

The Armourer says, but uncertainly now in the rich green light:
It is surely time to fire.

The Engineer replies with a hollowed and hardened voice and he gazes at The Armourer through two eyes that are now hag-stones. His speech has both the deep notes of bedrock and the bullety ting of flint flung on flint. The light in the Chapel is now a deep green, a moss green, the green where shadow meets leaf.

'Armourer, can you not see that we are being buried from the day?

We are down now past the plastic, the sea-coal, the flip-flops, down through the flints, the quartzites, the hags, and down to the imprint-taking, relic-yielding clay.

We are among bracelet clasps, spindle-whorls, a whale-bone table. We are among fossils: the mammoths, the turtles, the sharks, the nautilus, the wing bone of the albatross, the ear bone of the eagle ray.'

He pauses.

'Armourer, we are deep in matter, and this far down it
   is hard to transmit.
Messages can't make it, signals shatter.
Detonation is impossible.
Thought is, language is, turning to shingle.'

He pauses.

'Armourer,' says The Engineer – his lips are now chert,
   the slate blue of a peregrine's back and the sea's black
   before a storm, and his tongue is agate, all the profuse,
   unearthly colours of agate – 'I am petrified.'

The Armourer says, bringing at once a jollity and a fury to his voice:

Nevertheless, we have 'The Firing Song' to finish, and all
   are required to sing who are still fit for purpose.

'Oh happy band of pilgrims, drift upward to the
   skies
Where such a murmuration shall win so great a
   prize!

> *Song of the bomb, the drifting song,*
> *the firing song.*

Shingle shelters bunker, bunker shelters blast,
Dark drifts down, night flies fast.

Song of the wren, the devil-bird's song,
    the firing song.

A lichenous landscape mossing to green.
The king's in his cradle, the bomb's in its bay.

Song of the spores, the drifting song,
    the firing song.

Bedrock tightens from blue down to grey,
The final declension of world and of day.

Song of the hag, the sea-coal song, the
    firing song.

The ebb tide grades shingle finer then fine,
The fall-out settles soft to the pine.

Song of the bomb, the arming song,
    the firing song.'

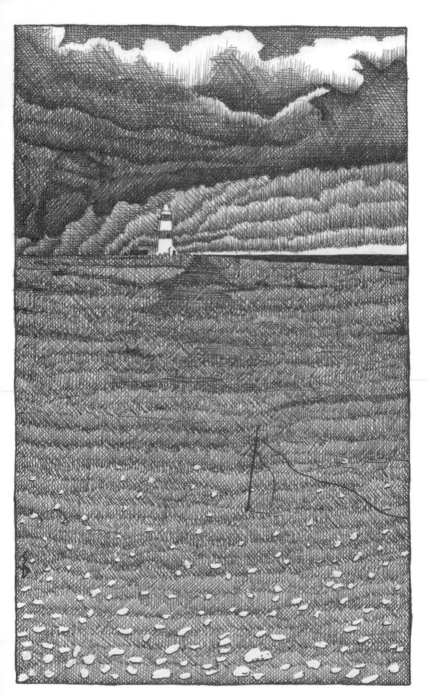

As

As is as thin as mist.

As is as fast as gale & as
slow as tar.

As moves as owls do, hushing through the air.

As moves as hyphae do,
slipping through the soil.

As is as light as ash & as bright as foil.

As is as heavy as mercury.

As is as scant as goodness in conditions of scarcity.

As is as massive as dark
matter.

As is as asymptote.

As is as nothingness.

As nears Ness.

As is hopelessness.

As is forgiveness.

As is Ness.

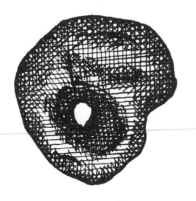

IN THE GREEN CHAPEL

VI

The Armourer says, against his better judgement, peering into the green gloom that is all around and within him:

It is as if there is no one there.

The Bryologist and The Physicist and The Engineer and The Ornithologist can no longer be seen in the green, and all that remains visible to The Armourer, who was once so sure of his vision, are the crosses, ten tall thin crosses on the west wall, and ten on the east, five on the north – and the south wall open to all that has now come through it.

The Armourer's hair is bracken, his innards are thickening peat, his back is clattered into a row of stones, his prick is soft and gilled as the Death Cap, foxes snarl in his blood, his tendons are all turned to high breaking-strain monofilament, all tuned to the wind-blown note of D flat, swifts scream through him on their hooligan tours, each of his ten nails is amber, his borders shift and re-form in each storm and he is Ness.

He sings a little to himself, though the voice is in no way any longer his:

> *'Song of Ness, the drifting song, the*
> *final song …'*

The bomb is buried beneath more layers of
    moss, more layers of moths.
The ferro-concrete is experiencing uncontrolled
    ruination.
Willow flourishes as forest, elder jungles
    each dip, each hollowness.
The falcon is bearing the day away.
The foreshore is moving as if it were alive,
    because it is alive.
Afternoon moonrise. Long light. Low sun.
    Slow dusk.
Shingle hush from distal to Ness.

it, he, she, they, as

It was all sea once, in a long unbroken line.

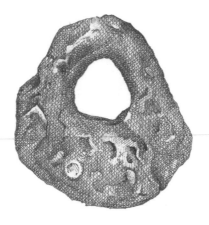

Holloway

In memory of

ROGER DEAKIN

1943–2006

Hol weg.

Holwy.

Holway.

Holeway.

Holewaye.

Hollowy.

Holloway.

Holloway – the hollow way. A sunken path, a deep & shady lane. A route that centuries of foot-fall, hoof-hit, wheel-roll & rain-run have harrowed into the land. A track worn down *by the traffic of ages & the fretting of water*, and in places *reduced sixteen or eighteen feet beneath the level of the fields.*

Holloways do not exist on the unyielding rock regions of the archipelago, where the paths stay high, riding the hard surface of the land. But where the stone is soft – malmstone, green-sand, sandstone, chalk – there are many to be found, some of them more ravines than roads.

They are landmarks that speak of habit rather than of suddenness. Like creases in the hand, or the wear on the stone sill of a doorstep or stair, they are the result of repeated human actions. Their age chastens without crushing. They relate to other old paths & tracks in the landscape – ways that still connect place to place & person to person.

Greenways, droveways, stanways, stoweys, bradways, white-ways, reddaways, radways, rudways, halsways, roundways, trods, footpaths, field-paths, leys, dykes, drongs, sarns, snickets, bostles, shutes, driftways, lichways, sandways, ridings, halter-paths, cartways, carneys, causeways, here-paths – & also fearways, dangerways, coffin-paths, corpseways & ghostways.

Many of those who have walked these old ways have seen them as places within which one might *slip back out of this world*, or within which ghosts softly flock. Edward Thomas spoke of hearing the voices of long-dead Roman soldiers as he walked an ancient trackway near Trawsfynydd in Wales. In Hampshire, where a stand of aspens whispered at the cross-roads of two old paths, he listened to the speech of a vanished village: *the ringing of hammer, shoe, & anvil* from the smithy, *the clink, the hum, the roar, the random singing* from the inn.

In 1689 the Japanese poet Basho followed his narrow path to the far north, & as he walked he spoke often with the long-dead poets of the past, including his twelfth-century forebear Saigyo, such that he came afterwards to describe his travels as conversations between *a ghost and a ghost-to-be*.

In 1937 the artist Eric Ravilious visited Gilbert White's parish of Selborne in Hampshire & walked the deep holloways that seam that landscape. He made an engraving of the entrance to one of the holloways – engraving itself a kind of track-making, an incision down into the box-wood or the copper – which shows the entrance to a deep lane, over which the trees are leaning & locking. This entrance to the underworld is guarded by a barn owl, white as the paper upon which it is printed. The owl's head is turned out towards the viewer – its eyes sentinel behind its knight's visor of feathers.

One need not be a mystic to accept that certain old paths are linear only in a simple sense. Like trees, they have branches &

like rivers they have tributaries. They are rifts within which time might exist as pure surface, prone to recapitulation & rhyme, weird morphologies, uncanny doublings.

Walking such paths, you might walk up strange pasts. This in the hunter's sense of 'walking up' – meaning *to flush out, to disturb what is concealed.*

The oldest holloways date back to the Iron Age. None is younger than 300 years old. Most holloways begin as ways to markets, to the sea, or to sites of pilgrimage, *lanes worn down by the packhorses of a hundred generations.* Some were boundary markers, & their routes therefore survive as word-maps in Anglo-Saxon charters:

> From the ford along the herepath to Wulfric's corner; & from the corner along the fence to the unknown watercourse, then to the bare stump; & from the bare stump along the fence to the great maple-tree, & then to the hedgerow apple-tree, & then to the herepath, & at last south to the holloway. Along the ditch south to the hollow watercourse, along the watercourse & up to the herepath, & along the herepath to the wheel ford once again.

Few holloways are in use now: they are too narrow and slow to suit modern travel, too deep to be filled in & farmed over. They exist – but cryptically. They have thrown up their own defences and disguises: nettles & briars guard their entrances, trees to either side bend over them & lace their topmost branches to form a tunnel or roof. On their sides, between the tree roots that snake *grotesque & wild*, grow the umbrals: hart's tongue fern, shining cranesbill, ivy & *moschatel, the lover of shade.*

This book is about a holloway & its shades, & a clear map of the holloway's finding is not contained within it.

In July 2004, I travelled with my friend Roger Deakin – swimmer; writer; naturalist; collector; worker with wood; writer of books; maker of friends – to explore the holloways of south Dorset.

These were among the things we carried with us: the novel *Rogue Male*, published by Geoffrey Household in 1939; a map of the area; two tents; a trenching tool; penknives (Roger's blunt, mine blunter); matches & candles; two hipflasks (one of whisky, one of arak).

The holloway we set out to find sits in the horseshoe of the Chideock Valley, cupped by *a half-moon of low green rabbit-cropped hills, the horns of which rest upon the sea.* The Chideock Valley sits within the Marshwood Vale. The Marshwood Vale sits within a further hoop of hills, rising to the high ground of Pilsdon Pen – a chalk summit of 277 metres, ringed by an Iron Age hill-fort.

Imagined from the north, therefore, from Pilsdon Pen, the Chideock holloway exists as a hollow set within a hollow set within a hollow – all of these hollows sloping south towards the sea & the shade of each in turn deepening the shade of the other.

Rogue Male was our guide to the holloway's location. Household's novel is about a man who – fleeing the mysterious pursuers intent on killing him – decides to go to ground in Dorset, somewhere in the half-moon of hills that encircle Chideock. He searches out a deep holloway that he had discovered earlier in his life, its bottom *a cart's width across &* its sides, *with the banks, the hedges above them, & young oaks leaping up front the hedge . . . were fifty feet of blackness.*

Anyone who wishes can dive under the sentinel thorns at the entrance, Household had written, *and push his way through . . . But who would wish?* It is, he warned, *a lane not marked on the map.*

Roger & I set out from the village of North Chideock to find Household's holloway. The blue July air hot & dry. Dust puffing from the road at our footfall; the smell of charred stone. Gold-blaze & rubber-shine from the yellow laurels that bordered the roads of North Chideock.

Only a few hundred yards from the car, where the tarmac began to run to its end, we found a small Catholic chapel of pale stone in the Romanesque style, set back amid oak trees. Roger pushed open its huge front door of ridged & bolt-studded oak. The door opened with an ease that belied its weight, its bottom edge gliding above the flagstones of the porch that were dipped and worn by the passage of many feet.

The air inside the church was cool, & the sandstone of its walls chill to the touch. There was a faint odour of must & everywhere the glint of gilt. Sun-pillars fell at a slant from high windows. *To Illuminate The Church, please place in meter slot £1 coin for 30 mins approx of light.*

The Chideock Valley has a recusant past. After the act of Supremacy in 1558 banned Catholic priests from Britain, missionaries began to re-infiltrate England to keep the faith alive. Several returned to the Chideock Valley & a high-stakes game of hide-&-seek began: the priests fugitive in the landscape, hiding in the woods & holloways; soldiers hunting for them & their supplicants.

The recusancy persisted for around fifty years. In the course of that half-century, five laymen & two priests were caught, tortured & executed. Among them was William Pike, *a simple country man & Chideock carpenter,* who was converted by Father Thomas Pilchard *& became his inseparable companion.* Arrested, tried as a convert & condemned as a traitor, during his execution Pike *was so strong that after he was cut down from the gibbet he stood up again & had to be thrust down & held by soldiers so that the butchery could continue.*

Hugh Green was arrested at Lyme Regis as he attempted to go to France, taken to Dorchester, tried & condemned. On 4 July 1642 he suffered *considerable barbarity, but remained conscious throughout the process of being hanged, drawn & quartered.* Eventually he was beheaded & *his head used as a football by the incensed mob.*

Father Cornelius ascended the scaffold at Dorchester, kissed the gallows, uttered the words of St Andrew – *O Cross, long desired* – *& prayed for his executioner & the queen* as the rope was placed around his neck.

Immediately after the execution of Father Pilchard, *Dorchester was beset with violent storms, which many took to be a judgement.*

We left the chapel & followed the road to its end & then picked up an old path leading into the hills, which was clearly the beginning of the holloway, for it was soon cut down ten feet or more into the caramel sandstone. Heavy rain had fallen the previous week & the holloway floor bore evidence of water-rush. Here & there patches of smooth surface stone had been rinsed clean & exposed, so that they lay glowing in their first sunlight for 200 million years.

Moving up into the hills, we checked & re-checked the descriptions in *Rogue Male*, but the landscape of the novel would not quite fit the landscape itself. There was a mismatch, slight but unmistakable. The directions of finding had been encrypted by Household.

Near the summit of the half-moon of hills, the path became so overgrown with nettles and brambles that we were unable to progress. We scrambled up its steep eastern side & into *the pollinous air of the flower meadow that bordered it*, from where the holloway we had been following was almost invisible. Then, by the side of a high old ash tree, we found a way back down into the holloway & so there we passed through that hole in the hedge & descended into the holloway's depth, using ivy as a rope to abseil down the sandstone sides & into the shade.

The bright hot surface world was forgotten. So close was the latticework of leaves & branches & so high the eastern side of the holloway that light penetrated its depths only in thin lances. We came occasionally to small clearings, where light fell & grass grew. In the windless warm air, groups of flies bobbed

& weaved, each dancing around a set point like vibrating atoms held in a matrix.

At one point we could see far along the holloway to the north, the curves of the walls holding the lens of empty light at its end. The view down a rifled barrel; an eye to the keyhole; a glimpse into the shade-world.

You could live undisturbed and undetected here for a long time, said Roger.

Later, after our first exploration of the main holloway, we set out on a wider reconnaissance of the area. We camouflaged our rucksacks with bracken & branch, climbed out of the holloway at the old ash tree & emerged into the meadow. The grass blades flashed like steel in the sun & we stood blinking & wringing the light from our eyes.

That afternoon we walked the curved ridge of hills that makes up the rest of the half-moon: Copper Hill, Denhay Hill, Jan's Hill. Everywhere we saw evidence of creatures taking refuge in the soil: mason bees, wasps, rabbits, successors to the fugitive priests & the hunted man. There were networks of burrows through the gorsy undergrowth: miniature green holloways, no bigger in cross-section than a croquet hoop, made by badgers.

Hours after, as the air was hazing up, we returned to our holloway hide-out, dropping down by the old ash-tree into the near-darkness. We cleared nettles and briars, moved loose trunks to make seats. We cut holly staffs with our penknives;

the fresh wood hard and pale to the blade. Roger built an almost smokeless fire with a hot centre of tinder, on which we cooked. Firelight flickered off the holloway walls & set complicated shadows moving in the leaves & the day seemed to convene itself about the furnace-point of the flames. We told stories, read out passages from *Rogue Male*. *I remind myself that I have extended and presumably will extend again in the time of the outer world.*

Down in the dusk of the holloway, the landscape's pasts felt excitingly alive & coexistent, as if history had pleated back on itself, bringing discontinuous moments into contact & creating correspondences that survived as a territorial imperative to concealment, escape & encounter.

After full nightfall, Roger & I pitched our tents on the flower meadow, behind a hedge & below the slope of Copper Hill & lay on our backs, looking up at the sky as the stars came fast & then faster. *A shooting star, there! Another, & then another.*

The next morning, a little after dawn, I climbed to the top of Copper Hill. There was an ocean of mist, filling the half-moon of hills & beyond the ocean of mist lay the sea itself to the south. The mist bred mirages of figures moving within it & the heat bred mirages over & upon the water, offering false promises of islands & mountain ranges.

Roger & I walked south and downhill, out of the holloway, off the half-moon of hills, down into the mist, past the chapel hidden in the laurels & down to the coast, where a pebble beach shelves steeply away from high sandstone cliffs.

The sea was warm so we swam, backstroking out for a hundred yards or so & then treading water. We looked back at the ochre sandstone cliffs & the green hills rising behind them & our arms and legs moving like phantom limbs beneath the surface of the blue, blue sea.

In August 2006, Roger died. He died many years too young. The day of his death I went with two friends to the pine-forests of Holkham in North Norfolk. The light in the deepest stands of the pines was like dusk, and the air smelt resinous, spicy. We slept among the trees & at dawn and dusk we walked across the gold & open beach to swim in big, steady waves. For miles along the wrack-line lay razor-shells in their millions.

In September 2011, I returned to the Dorset holloway with two friends, Dan Richards & Stanley Donwood.

These were among the things we carried: a copy of Geoffrey Household's *Rogue Male*. The map that Roger & I had taken to the holloway. Two rucksacks & a pair of saddle-bags, a hip-flask, two penknives, matches & candles. A bottle of damson gin.

We parked at Pilsdon Pen & walked through Lob Gate, steeply up towards the summit of the Pen. White chalk, sharp flint, the purple of ling, the green of gorse & yellow stars of tormentil. Halfway up its slopes we passed into a thick & enfolding mist which we had not seen from its base & within that mist we each swiftly became a ghost to the other.

There were times, as I walked the ramparts of the hill fort widdershins, Stan walked them deasilwise & Dan stepped across their centre, when each of us moved lost in our own luminous socket of mist & there were times when we showed as silhouettes & times when our paths crossed & we emerged into focus, before shifting away again.

Once, I dropped down into the wide path that ran between the ramparts, the path that was sunk down within them & to which they provided the walls & I experienced the powerful illusion that the path was sloping away and downhill ahead of me & not running to an end or continuing its own progress, but rather fraying down & out into the mist & offering an invitation to descend.

From Pilsdon Pen it was down, steeply down, into the Marshwood Vale & from the Marshwood Vale it was up, steeply up, on high-sided lanes, until at last we found a path across the ridge of the west side of *the half-moon of hills* & that path felt like a borehole through the ridge rather than a passage over it, for it was so overgrown that it was more tunnel than path. We emerged out of its darkness into the Chideock Valley & almost immediately Dan fell off his bike & then stood up laughing from the verge.

That long & happy day passed in exploration, tree-climbing, walking, talking, lounging. I had not gone in search of Roger's shade, but I found him there nonetheless, glimpsed startlingly clearly at the turn of a corner or the edge of a tree-line. Actual memory traces existed in the stumps of the holly saplings we had cut as staffs, our blade-marks still visible in the wood. *He knowth hym by the traces & by his denne and by the soole.*

I now understand it certainly to be the case, though I have long imagined it to be true, that stretches of a path might carry memories of a person just as a person might of a path.

In the flower meadow below Copper Hill, near an old flat oak, I read out poems by Edward Thomas, who was the great twentieth-century poet of the old way, as Paul Nash was its great twentieth-century artist. Thomas walked thousands of miles along paths, from the famous (Sarn Helen in Wales, the Icknield Way & the Ridgeway in the chalk counties of southern England) to the local (Old Litton Lane & Harepath Lane, near his Hampshire home). His poems are thronged with ghosts, doubles & paths that peter out. He understood himself in topographical terms & he saw that paths run through people as surely as they run through places.

Many a road and track
That, since the dawn's first crack,
Up to the forest brink,
Deceived the travellers
Suddenly now blurs
And in they sink.

– o –

Late that night, we cycled back up to the holloway in fierce silver rain, skidding on wet mud, raindrops showing in our headlamp beams & the eye-glow of unknown animals glinting in the hedgerows.

The eyes of creatures shine in low light because of the presence of the *tapetum lucidum,* the bright carpet, a mirror-like membrane of iridescent cells that sits behind the retina. Light passes first through the rod & cone cells then strikes the membrane & rebounds back through the retina towards the light source. Any available light is used twice to see with; perception is thereby doubled.

So heavy was the rain and so thick the blackness of the night, that we soon became separated, each invisible to the other & yet when we later spoke, each of us had had the experience of being pursued by another who was not of our group – someone holding a bright light & following in our tracks.

We slept that night down in the depths of the holloway. In the darkest hours of the night a rain storm came, the water falling so hard it left drill-holes in the leaf-litter. Waking at dawn I found that I had left my copy of Edward Thomas's poems unsheltered. The rain had plumped it & driven gobbets of earth & shards of leaf in between its pages:

The path, winding like silver, trickles on,
Bordered and even invaded by thinnest moss
. . . and the eye
Has but the road, the wood that overhangs
And underyawns it, and the path that looks
As if it led on to some legendary
Or fancied place where men have wished to go
And stay; till, sudden, it ends where the wood ends.

After full sunrise we walked and bicycled down to the coast at Seatown & there we climbed Ridge Cliff and Doghouse Hill in a high & golden light & a strong white wind. We climbed them barefoot, fitting our feet into the print-trails that had been dipped into the turf by earlier walkers, & the earth was warm and finely graded within each print. To our west was the Undercliff, & Lyme Regis round the bay. White-sailed yachts scooted eastwards on the big wind; Stan's hat was snatched from his head by the wind.

Later that day, before we left the valley, we went to the Catholic chapel in North Chideock. In the visitors' book had been written many prayers & supplications.

29/08/2010 *Please bless Lisa Bevely who was murdered leaving her little boy of five years. Thank you.*

17-July-2011 *Pray for my two friends who are ill, Joshua Davies and Sue Holloway.*

25th August '10 *Please bless a good friend who has not long left us, may he rest in peace.*

PILSDON PEN

Looking out from the lower turf ramparts of Pilsdon Pen we sight a crescent moon of hills – a vein within a leaf spring – arcing to the coast. Somewhere in there lies our quarry; a lane diving into the dark.

An inky eye, an ammonite.
A hollow, foot-querned way.

Turning away from the sea we begin to scale the hill. Over the stile, spiralling up between tussocks and gorse, stepping through the sudden cloud-line into thickly mantled murk. A lichen souper. Up until we clamber out on a floating island steppe – a layered mist rolling about our three glades in the fog. There is a trig: there, silent cattle; here, earthworks – mounds and humps.

All elsewhere is milk.
A void.

We spread out to search our margins: Rob to the left, Stan to the right, me down the middle of the dim flat top. We do not orchestrate this trident sweep but each, finding himself alone, determines to carry on through the ether, round the worked ellipse, skirting the moat, to the point we'll surely converge . . . on the edge of the fern-table brume.

A fume quoit caught on this whittled marl peg.

Walking out purblind, vision penned and closing down –
sapped, as a migraine pinches the light – I can hear nothing
but the damp air pool and pass, tendril fog-weed fringing-in to
clag my ears in unnatural silence. I stump on.

Then I begin to see things. I hear the doldrum sirens call – fine
and far away.
There.

Beguiling; warm; inviting; sad.
Strange; familiar.

'Where are my friends?' I ponder, vaguely. 'How long have I
been...'

Then I fall off the world.

Back down in the particular we unstrap our bikes.

The car. That strap. My bike. This. The tactile reassurance of the
close at hand. Sunlight falls and kestrels call to disavow what we'd
just seen and been through and, indeed, the clouds seem to have
lifted off and melted quite away when we turn and look back.

Stan and I plunge down the brink and speed. The rifled lanes
spill past and we grin tight until, turn approaching, brakes
applied – and now, and now; no, come on; now – I begin a
slow crash into Dorset with its gleaming chalk and plough-
turned flint-tipped ruts.

HOLLOWAY

Sat above the dry den shute in a silver flat-grained dusk, I listen to the others talking – out of sight, away down in the dip. Yesterday, we hid our belongings in the pleats of the old road's bed – the bicycles and bivvy bags half-buried in the drifts of blanket mulch.

My bicycle did not take well to the rough farm tracks and bridle-ways. Tyres too thin, gears too high – a frail old race-horse forced to plough – soon the chain was broken and the gears bent out of shape . . . Maybe I should have abandoned it here, I thought; lost on a long-forgotten road – black frame left to flake and moulder under trunks grown pinguid-fat round broken old barbed wire.

It is late September and the day is mostly ebbed.

This morning we ate tea-bread and drank violet damson gin from the bottle. We stretched and yawned, the sleep still in our eyes, flat earth smell on our hands. Waking in the holloway the thing that struck me, lying half out of my green cocoon and staring up – staring through the awning mesh of twigs and stems – was the way their patterns shone white when I blinked or turned away. A fretted photo-negative weaving with the vessels in my eye.

Burnt in. Of a piece.

Once up, we sat round in the bank, ears pricked. We slept well but for the rain at four, faintly aware of the bird song swell with the sun – the hedges here are stuffed with birds; abundant, loud and brazen-bright as we are out of place. We hide ourselves as émigrés, as artificers in a trench, sat with our sub rosa gin below the parapet.

Some 250 miles east, in an archive box, I found a card:

As an only child, the sheer solitude of the hero's escape and odyssey appealed to me. He was a swimmer too, dragged his tortured body into the Rhine like an otter – throwing off the guard-dogs that pursued him.

Down in the next valley's pub, we sit beside the cheerful fire and talk: nursing pints, mindful of the cold outside and the dark walk home to our deep burrow sacks.

On the way back, I recall the lady stood on the hill behind our hide whose blank stare caught and pinned us as we climbed into the world this morning, whilst her dog – quite forgotten – ran circles. Her red jacket, madder red – her frown of vexed mistrust.

Later, three lights dazzle up and we all start and scramble into the ditch, for fear of lamping, hardwired fright of the hunted, the trees shot through and blazing – men come to pick us off.

Yet, when we woke again next day – everything as it should be; three men in a hedge – we agreed the episode seemed spectral and unreal. A shared night terror dreamt up in the wake of old ale dregs . . . but what of these scuffed marks, here; these hurried flails cut in the fosse? These thrashing breaks for cover in the boundary of the bank?

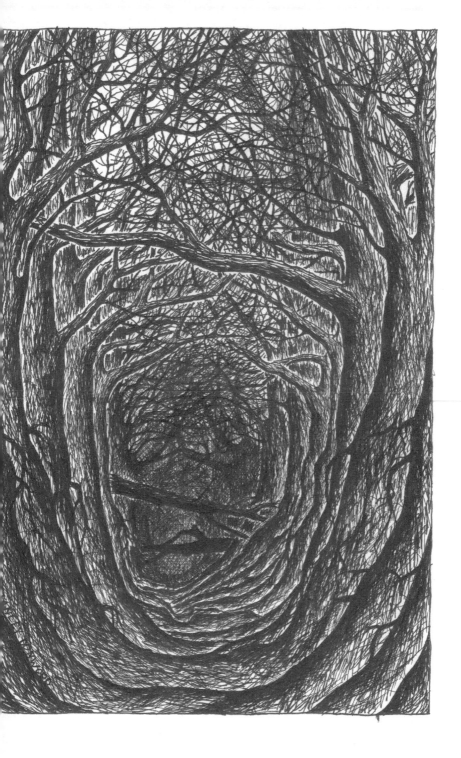

MARTYRS

The bees that tunnel in the rock and hard-packed mud of the
walls here go back a long way.

Holed-up underneath the thread-work of the vaulting ash, thin
holly, beech and suckered elms – sinew peeling, shot through
with poison galleries – I peer into the bee maze, stood down
among the rib roots and moss.

The bees still mass in the *hola weg* and drone down in the valley church, the gilded Queen of martyrs, beside the aged books
and pitch mantraps.

Records of steel barbs in the hollow, hooded troops cast out
to snare a covert congregation – creeping round the black-
wood crescent; lamping with dark lanterns. No moon above
the whispering fields, low service in the cross-hatched apse and
every outside sound an ambush. Amphidromic points of faith.

The holloway is absence; a wood-way worn away by buried feet. Regressing back into the mind, an ink-preoccupation set amongst the forests of Northern Europe and the bright beast tapestry of the hunt. Walking, hiding, running man, huddled in the lee of a tree – a tree amongst trees, a way among ways – brief safety in the sunken lull. Flayed into tingling life by the hopeless desire to love.

In the burnished little church, four hollow men gaze out to us from flaking plaster frescos. Becher silo faces.

Stark, composed – but one's eyes focus off, preoccupied – as if by bees.

Hol weg.

Holwy.

Holway.

Holeway.

Holewaye.

Hollowy.

Holloway.